Where do you think your political views are right now?

How do you believe the US should conduct itself when it comes to interational affairs? Are we really the policemen of the world, or should we allow other countries to do as they please while we mind our own business?

If China or Russia wanted to set up a military base on US soil, would they be free to do so? After all, the US has bases all over the world.

The War on Drugs has been costly and filled our prisons with people who will likely have no future due to a criminal record. What is your solution to this problem, or do you see it as a success?

In the balance between States' rights and the federal government, which one do you feel should have the most power?

It's possible to eliminate the national income tax, but only if you redefine and shrink the role of the federal government. Is this a good idea?

Homosexual marriage was legalized at the federal level. Do you believe the federal government should be involved in marriage? Is it a State right? Or should it be left to religious institutions and not politicized at all?

Do you believe parents should have the right to homeschool their children? Why or why not?

North Korea is an Orwellian nightmare. Her people have endured torture, spying, starvation, public executions, and more. Moreover, North Korea likes to threaten her neighbors as well as the US. How would you solve this problem?

Mass killings have become a recent problem. Some blame guns, some blame psychiatric meds, some blame video games, and others society as a whole. How do you propose we curb this surge in violence?

The War on Terror was undeclared and hasn't officially ended yet. The US has systematically invaded and destabilized much of the Middle East. How would you plan to either continue or end this lengthy war?

Despite all the bills and reforms, many Americans still cannot afford health insurance. Do you have a solution that would bring better healthcare to more people?

Religious texts, such as the 10 Commandments, are no longer permitted to hang in schools or courthouses. Should this be permissible?

Should the Pledge of Allegiance be mandatory in school? Why or why not?

Is it too disrespectful to sit during the National Anthem, or is it simply a strong political statement?

Should transgender students be allowed to share locker rooms and the like
with students who are bioligically their preferred sex? Should they have their
own facilities? Should they use the biologically appropriate ones?

Should transgender athlethes be allowed to compete on the sports teams of their choice?

Canada and the USA have very strict immigration rules, even if you just plan to visit. It's promoting illegal immigration from poorer countries. How do we resolve the issues with her boarders?

As of right now, there are thousans of people living illegally in the US. Many of them are having children here, making those children American citiziens by birth. What do we do about this problem, or is it not a problem?

How do you feel about the current value of the dollar? Is it fine, or should we be aiming for further inflation or perhaps deflation instead?

Travel to and from Canada has gotten extremely strict. Should be have open boarders with Canada?

The near total destabilization of the Middle East has left many people displaced and seeking refuge in the Western world. This coincides with a growing number of terrorist sects within US cities. What's the solution?

The US has the highest number of prisoners in the world as well as the highest recidivism rate. How do we solve this problem?

The United States has long, harsh prison sentences. Norway has an incredibly low recidivism rate, imposes "soft" sentences, and believes in rehabiliation over retribution. Is this a good model? Why or why not?

Despite a massive protest from the Sioux tribe as well as many others, the Dakota Access Pipeline was built and is operational. Should it have been disbanded? Why or why not?

As the world looks to undercut oil companies with clean energy, what is the proper role of government concerning such a thing? Should it be federally funded, or rely on grassroots funding?

Which do you value more: safety or freedom? Why?

As the human population expands, many species are becoming endangered and extinct, mostly due to habitat destruction. How do we protect both the diversity of species on Earth without compromising human rights?

The quest to find habitable planets and ways to reach them is ongoing. If we had the means to colonize such a planet, how should the government(s) respond?

Science is on the verge of slowing, stopping, and even reversing aging. Perpetual youth is on the horizon, and with it comes the reduction of many diseases, such as Alzheimer's. Is this something the government should be funding?

Some people are frustrated, believing they may not get a job they applied for or a college grant they want because of the push to hire more women and minorities. Is it justified, or should we take a different approach?

The Democratic party is embracing socialism more and more, with many candidates openly calling themselves socialists. How do you respond to this? Embrace it? Reject it?

Fears that Yellowstone may erupt seem to be growing. Should the government fund efforts to stabilize it?

Some people would like to dismantle America's two-party system, leveling the playing field for third party candidates. Should voters be more exposed to and open towards these political ideologies? Should they have a better chance?

Which is more important to you when it comes to electing a politician: good moral character or shrewed politics and loyalty to the party? Is there middle ground? What do you think?

Describe your ideal governor. What's his or her platform? Does he or she raise or lower taxes to complete his or her agenda?

Describe your ideal President of the United States? How does the country change under his or her leadership?

Should preschool become mandatory education? Do parents raise children, or does the State? Is there middle ground, or should parents be solely responsible for children?

Should the federal government be setting guidelines for school lunches? Michelle Obama's reforms not only sparked protests from students, but the companies that provide the food had difficulties with the new regulations.

Japan is one of the safest countries around, but at a price. Teachers police the streets at night to make sure students are at home and not running around, and police routinely stop people. Is such a price worth a low crime rate?

Should abortion be legal? Why or why not? What about a woman's rights?
What about the unborn baby's rights?

Finland has one of the highest ranked educations in the world. Children don't start school until age 7, most work is done in the classroom instead of at home, and get 75 minutes of recess. Would this work in America?

As of 2018, the United States still has no official language. Should one or more
be adopted, or is it better as it is?

Climate change has become a political issue. Do you believe it's predominately man-made, or a natural cycle? Should the government be doing something about it, and if so, what?

Do you believe in term limits for congressmen and women? Why would it be or not be beneficial?

People spent the 2016 election cycle wondering whether Hillary Clinton's actions were worthy of a prison sentence or if she was simply doing what all politicians do. What's your take?

Is the Confederate flag offensive to you? Should the government be involved in either preserving or shaping America's cultural heritage?

Some extremists advocated for revoking the Women's Suffrage Act, arguing that since men gave women their rights, they can take them away. Should women's rights be natural, like a man's, or a priviledge extended by men?

Some politicians blamed violent video games for certain school shootings. Should the sale and ratings of video games be controlled by the State, or is it up to parents to monitor what media their kids consume?

As President, George W. Bush weilded a lot of emergency power. Obama expanded those powers. Should such power ever be granted, or does it upset the balance between the POTUS, Congress, and the courts too much?

How do you interpret the seperation of Church and State? Is it to protect the State from a particular relgion's influence? Is it to shield religions from the tyranny and prejudice of the State? Both? Or should it be done away with?

Donald Trump believes that imposing tariffs will rebuild some of America's traditional industries? Do you agree with him? If not, how would you approach the same problem?

Did you identify or participate in Tea Party protests? Why or why not? Do you think it accomplished anything?

Did you instead participate in Occupy Walstreet protests? Why or why not? Did it accomplish anything?

Some have said that foreign aid does nothing but take money from poor Americans and give it to rich people in poor countries. Others believe foreign aid does much good. What say you?

Some commentators have compared the current United States to Rome. Rome was once a Republic until Julius Ceasar turned the tide. Eventually Rome became a monarchy. Is the US at risk of such a thing?

We hear of business owners refusing service to people for whatever reason. They might be gay, wearing a MAGA hat, or practicing a religion they don't agree with. Do they have the right to refuse service?

With BREXIT, Britian is due to be leaving the European Union. Is such a move a good one, or are we past the point of clinginig to national sovereignty?

What's your opinion on government bailouts? Are there any banks or companies too big to fail? What do bailouts do to our currency?

Do you believe that we should continue to make nuclear weapons, or that they should remain on the table during times of conflict?

Are there any dystopian stories' warnings you feel American's should heed a little closer. <u>1984, Hunger Games, V for Vendetta, The Running Man</u>?

Some comedians refuse to perform at college campuses because the current generation can't take a joke. Are we too politically correct? Is it good that we're more sensitive, or is it causing backlash?

Do you believe that Americans in general still have a Cold War mentality towards Russia? Should we be trying to repair relations, or is Russia simply a rougue nation that needs to learn its place?

Some say that American politicians across the board have been bought by Israeli lobbies. Is it important that America stand by Israel? Why?

Israel often justifies its actions towards Palestinian aggression as exercising Israel's right to exist. The question is, does any government or nation have the right to exist? Do governments have rights? Did Rome? Prussia?

What would be the ideal America? What would be its major strength?

Child labor is a huge problem in China, and Americans are often accused of enabling it through our purchasing and outsourcing habits. Is it a problem we should be concerned about? If it is, what would you do?

Some companies are working on lab grown meat. Such a thing would cut down massively on CO2 and cut back on the number of fields we need. Unfortunately, it would put ranchers virtually out of business. How should we address it?

At the start of every major conflict, talk of the dreaded draft starts up again. Should we abolish it permanently, ruling it unconstitutional? Should females not be exempt from it?

There have been politicians making the case to return to the gold or silver standard, ensuring that our currency is backed by something substantial instead of a fiat currency. Would this be a good idea?

Which economic theory do you prefer: Keynesian or Austrian?

In the aftermath of 9/11, we've seen the rise of the TSA, Patriot Act, and much more surveilance in general. Are these necessary, or has government overrreached?

Many graduates are buried under the crushing debt of student loans. The price of education has gone up, and it seems that everyone is pushing for a degree. How can we alleviate the burden?

Some schools are dropping cursive handwriting from the curriculum. Is that a good idea, or is cursive a useful tool?

Some states are considering banning certain dog breeds. Others have a ban on a number of 'exotic' animals. What's your opinion? Should people be allowed to own what they want? Should they need training first?

Who was your favorite POTUS? If you could, would you re-elect him as President of of modern-day America?

Let's make it more interesting. If you could elect any ruler throughout history, whether king or queen, emperor or empress, prime minister, tsar or tsarina, etc., who would you like?

Should the United States leave the UN? Is the UN an asset to the world?

In Minnesota, the moose population is falling due to the artificially high number of deer, as they carry a parasite harmful to moose. Should hunters have to back off while the population recovers, or should the moose just be driven off?

The Federal Reserve, which control the currency, is actually not a government entity. It has resisted all attempts to see their innter workings. Should it be regulated and audited?

Which fictional society would you like to live in? What makes it so appealing
to you?

Some say the electoral college is necessary to make sure each area is represented fairly and the most populated cities don't single-handedly determine elections. Others believe it should be determined by popularity alone. You?

When Michelle Obama became First Lady, she began making changes to, for example, the school lunch program. Should an unelected person have the power to make such broad changes or any at all?

In the world of microaggressions and cultural appropriation, should be concerned about freedom of speech and freedom of expression?

Do you believe racism and/or sexism has increased over the past 10 or so years? If so, do you believe it was caused by our current political climate, or has it always existed and is contributing to our current political climate?

Signs that say things like "All Lives Matter" and "It's Okay to be White" are hailed by some as promoting pride in yourself and heritage no matter what, while others say it's hateful. Where do you stand?

Donald Trump recently cut foreign aid to Puerto Rico on the basis that they aren't using to rebuild their infrastructure but are just distributing it among the wealthy. Do you agree with him? Are we obligated to continue sending money?

Ron Paul once wrote, "Truth is treason in the Empire of lies." Do you agree with the government's persecution of whistleblowers and leaks, such as those who contribute to Wikileaks?

On that note, do you believe Edward Snowden is a hero or a traitor? What should his punishment be, if any?

Is it the President's job to run the country? Where should his or her limits lie, and should Presidents be reluctant to seek extra power?

Who makes the best politicians? Those who have an interest in it and work their way from mayor to governor and higher, or are nonpoliticians the best, for they are used to trying to live a 'normal' life?

Some people are pushing to make preschool mandatory. Do you believe this is a good idea or is it pushing kids into the system way too young?

We've heard both heroic victories and sheer horror stories coming from social services' involvement in the lives of children and the elderly. Do you believe these departments are too far-reaching and corrupt?

Do you believe there was any way to avoid the Civil War? Was it necessary to save the Union and abolish slavery, or could different steps have been taken to acheive the same or a similar outcome?

Which war do you think was America's last "good war?" What good has come
from it? What bad?

Should Spanish be a mandatory language in schools or should it remain an elective?

With Disney acquiring multiple IPs and properties some people have been wondering if the laws on monopoly should be revised? Do you agree or disagree?

How should the various governments (both Federal and local) respond to natural disasters?

Is standardized testing an asset to schools or does it force teachers to spend too much time teaching kids how to pass tests?

Where do you think you stand politically after all these questions? Did any of your answers surprise you?